People of Destiny

A Humanities Series

There comes a time,
we know not when,
that marks
the destiny of men.

Joseph Addison Alexander

People of Destiny

ERNEST HEMINGWAY

By Norman Richards

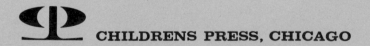 CHILDRENS PRESS, CHICAGO

The editors wish to express
their appreciation to Mr. Meyer Goldberg,
who created the series and inspired
the publication of People of Destiny.

Cover and body design: John Hollis

Project editor: Joan Downing

Assistant editor: Elizabeth Rhein

Illustrations: John Hollis and Ron Kangles
—Hollis Associates

Research editor: Robert Hendrickson

Photographs: From the files of Wide World
Photos, Inc., and Atlantic-Little, Brown
and Co.

Typesetting: American Typesetting Co.

Printing: Regensteiner Press

Quotation on page 12 from DEATH IN THE AFTERNOON
by Ernest Hemingway, reprinted by permission of the executors
of the Ernest Hemingway estate and the publishers, Charles
Scribner's Sons, New York, and Jonathan Cape, Ltd., London.

Photographs on pages 15, 16, 18, 20, 21, 22, 25, 27, 32, and 36-37
from AT THE HEMINGWAYS: A FAMILY PORTRAIT
by Marcelline Hemingway Sanford, by permission of Atlantic-
Little, Brown and Co. Copyright © 1961, 1962 by Marcelline
Hemingway Sanford.

Contents

Danger in Africa

The small, four-seat Cessna airplane skimmed over the African landscape at a low altitude. The pilot scanned the horizon ahead as the two passengers, Mr. and Mrs. Ernest Hemingway, peered down, looking for Victoria Falls on the river below.

The world-famous author, with his wife, had been hunting leopards and lions deep in British East Africa, far from civilization. He had embarked on the hunting trip for two reasons: to enjoy a sport that had been a lifelong passion, and to experience and understand the feelings of a hunter on foot in the dark of night, in danger of being attacked. This was the first time he had hunted at night in this kind of country, and he wanted to be able to describe the experience in the penetrating fashion that marked all his writing. He had gotten his wish when a lion, wounded by a spear, had charged at him; he had shot it at close range.

The engine of the chartered plane droned as it winged over the countryside. Suddenly a great flock of ibis birds rose in the plane's path, coming head on.

"Hang on!" the pilot yelled as he shoved the control yoke forward. Instantly the plane went into a steep dive, plunging down and narrowly missing

---

A wounded lion is extremely dangerous to hunters in the African jungles. Hunting at night, Hemingway is attacked by such a lion, but manages to shoot it at close range.

9

the birds. As the ground rushed up at the plane, the pilot pulled back on the yoke, just managing to pull the craft out of the dive in time.

Now he jammed the throttle forward, applying the full power of the plane's lone engine in an attempt to climb. He saw the telephone wire strung between rotting poles in the split second before the aircraft struck it and lurched toward the ground. Fighting to keep the craft in level flight, he pulled hard at the controls as the plane plummeted. It struck the ground hard, but in the correct landing position, then ripped through the underbrush and skidded to a stop.

The pilot muttered a prayer of relief as the Hemingways struggled out of the battered cabin. Ernest was only bruised, but his wife, Mary, had suffered two cracked ribs. The pilot was unhurt.

The trio decided to spend the night on the ground near the plane, then strike out for help the next day. It was a rough night. The Hemingways' pain kept them awake, and several huge elephants, disturbed at their presence, trumpeted loudly and came within a few yards of trampling them. It was a relief when morning came and the beasts went away.

Undaunted, the trio began walking along a riverbank early in the morning. By a stroke of luck, a launch cruised up the river that day and they hailed it. The operator took them to the small settlement of Butiaba, where there was an airport, and they chartered another plane for a flight back to their base of operations in Kenya. The little plane roared down the runway, rose uncertainly into the air, sputtered—and suddenly crashed. It hit the ground with considerable impact and, seconds later, burst into a mass of flames.

This time Hemingway was seriously injured, but he struggled to help his wife out of the plane, and all three occupants managed to escape before the craft became an inferno. The rugged, fifty-five-year-old author had suffered serious internal injuries, damage to his spine, and a concussion. Luckily, immediate help was available in the nearby village. From there he was taken by automobile to a medical facility in a larger town.

In the meantime, the wreckage of the first airplane had been sighted in the wilderness by search planes, and it was assumed that Hemingway was dead. The news went out to world, and newspapers in every country carried the dispatch. Headlines read: HEMINGWAY MEETS VIOLENT END IN AFRICA and ADVENTUROUS AUTHOR DIES AS HE LIVED. Most papers carried obituaries summarizing his life, and millions of people were shocked and saddened.

Ernest Hemingway was one of that handful of writers whose names have become household words in countries throughout the world. His career had been capped recently by the almost unanimous critical acclaim for his book, *The Old Man and the Sea*, for which he had been awarded the Pulitzer Prize in 1953. Even people who never read distinguished literature were familiar with his books, for several of them had been made into movies that were seen

Elephants, upset at the presence of strangers at night, come near to trampling the Hemingways and their pilot as the three sleep on the ground near their crashed plane in Uganda.

by millions of people. *A Farewell to Arms, To Have and Have Not, For Whom the Bell Tolls, The Snows of Kilimanjaro,* and *The Killers* were some of his famous works that were adapted for films.

Hemingway's life had been one of adventure, danger, high spirits, and zest. It was also distinguished by hard work, honesty, and an almost fanatical struggle toward artistic perfection. He had known hunger and poverty in his early days of writing, but he had refused to change his approach and write solely for financial gain. The world had finally realized that he was creating an original literature, and along with public acclaim, he had eventually achieved financial success. Now, at the height of his fame, it appeared that the writer had courted danger once too often.

But the action-packed life of Ernest Hemingway had not yet run its course. Virtually every newspaper in the world reported his survival in banner headlines the next day when the news was flashed out of Africa. HEMINGWAY ALIVE! The front pages shouted the joyous words from every newsstand. Newspaper accounts had him striding jauntily from the jungle, making light of his narrow escape.

In truth, Hemingway was seriously concerned about his injuries and was thankful to be alive. His flair for the colorful and dramatic, however, showed itself in his remarks.

"My luck, she is running good," he said to newsmen at one point, and he avoided discussing his injuries in detail in subsequent interviews.

This harrowing incident in Africa was only one of many dramatic chapters in Hemingway's life—a life in which he frequently found that his every action was noticed by the world. He did not always seek the spotlight, and he often resented the interruptions in his work that resulted from his fame. He was, however, not only one of the twentieth century's greatest writers but a living symbol of literary success. He could no more have avoided this destiny than he could have settled for less than perfection in his writing.

A riverboat, as shown above, picks up the Hemingways and their pilot the morning after their first plane crash. Right, a family reunion after the two plane crashes. Left to right: Hemingway, his son John, and his wife Mary.

A Solid Beginning

Ernest Hemingway's colorful life as a writer and an adventurer was in sharp contrast to the life he had known as a child. The first son of a solid, respectable, middle-class family, he grew up in Oak Park, Illinois, a suburb of Chicago. It was an ordinary environment, although the Hemingway family was a little better off than most American families in the early years of this century.

The Hemingways were an old New England family who moved to Chicago when Ernest's grandfather, Anson, was still a child. Anson T. Hemingway grew up to be a serious, religious man who was a general secretary of the YMCA for many years. He then started a real estate business in Oak Park. His son, Clarence Edmonds Hemingway, was a sensitive boy who loved animals and the beauty of nature. Having decided early in life to become a doctor, he went to medical school when the time came and then settled down to practice in Oak Park.

It was in these comfortable circumstances that he married a local girl, Grace Hall, in 1896. Her father, Ernest Hall, had been born and raised in England, and had prospered in the cutlery business after moving to Chicago. Grace, like her mother, was passionately interested in music and had studied voice and piano for years. She had thought seriously of a career in music, but gave it up to marry the eligible young Oak Park physician.

For the first several years of their marriage, the Clarence Hemingways lived in her father's big Victorian house. The Hemingway family home was directly across the street, and the two families spent much of their time together. They nearly always had maids and other household help in this age of

Hemingway's birthplace at 439 (now 339) North Oak Park Avenue, Oak Park, Illinois.

low-cost labor, and life was pleasant and well-ordered.

The Hemingways' first child, Marcelline, was born in 1898 and was followed a year later by Ernest, who was born on July 21, 1899. Another daughter, Ursula, was born three years afterward, and another, Madelaine, two years after that. The last child, Leicester, didn't come into the world until Ernest was sixteen years old.

Young Ernest Hemingway enjoyed a boisterous, happy boyhood in the peaceful town of Oak Park. He was a lively, energetic child with a vivid imagination, who delighted in telling tall tales from the time he learned to talk. This sometimes upset his parents, who scolded him for "lying."

Dr. Hemingway initiated Ernest into the world of nature at an early age. He took him for long walks through fields and woods, pointing out plants, flowers, and animals. He took the boy fishing almost as soon as he could walk, and Ernest quickly picked up his father's love for this pastime. It was to stay with him for the rest of his life.

Ernest was still a toddler when his parents built a summer cottage on the shore of Walloon Lake, near Petoskey, Michigan, some three hundred miles from Chicago. The family spent its summers there from the time the cottage was built, continuing the custom long after the children had grown up. Some of the happiest days of Ernest's life were spent in that rural environment he learned to love.

He spent hours roaming the woods to hunt possums, woodchucks, and porcupines as soon as he was old enough to shoot a gun. He became so proficient at fishing that the family photo albums soon filled up with snapshots of Ernest displaying his catches.

The Hemingways tried to give their children a sense of responsibility. Each member of the family was given chores to do regularly. Ernest's tasks included walking to a nearby farm every day to get jars of milk. He also had to rake the beach, sweep the porch, and perform any odd jobs that his parents requested.

Two early photographs of the Hemingway family. Top, left to right: Ursula, Dr. Hemingway, Ernest, Mrs. Hemingway, and Marcelline, in 1903. Bottom, left to right: Ernest, Ursula, and Marcelline, with Grandfather Hall, in 1904.

Ernest was not yet of school age when his grandfather Hall died, leaving a considerable amount of money to Ernest's mother. A strong, determined woman who made many of the family's important decisions, she now decided to use the money to buy a new home. She designed a large, fifteen-room stucco house and ordered it built. The house was to have a special two-story high music room with a balcony, for concerts and voice recitals—the kind of room she had dreamed of having for years.

Mrs. Hemingway was determined that each of her children learn music, and she launched them into voice lessons as well as lessons on various instruments. She chose the cello for Ernest, and made him practice every day of the week, even though he hated it and showed little talent. He continued the lessons for years, dreading the hour he spent alone each afternoon in the music room. He was also enrolled in the children's choir at church, which his mother directed, and for awhile he was the boy soprano soloist.

Ernest, however, was too much of an outdoor boy to enjoy music the way his mother had hoped he would. He especially loved shooting clay pigeons with his father, and was a good shot at an early age. This was a favorite Sunday activity for the whole family during the summers at Walloon Lake. A 20-gauge shotgun received on his tenth birthday from Grandfather Hemingway became Ernest's most treasured possession.

He found a new way to use the music room when his mother wasn't around. It made an excellent boxing arena, and when Ernest and his schoolmates had disagreements, he would bring them to

---

Far left, Ernest's mother shows her children a large fish she caught at Walloon Lake. Ernest is at her right. Left, Ernest and a friend hunt in the Michigan woods, using shotguns.

Early photographs of the Hemingways. Far left, left to right standing: Ernest, Madelaine, Marcelline, Ursula; seated: Dr. Hemingway, with Carol on his lap, and Mrs. Hemingway. Left: Ernest with a woodchuck at Walloon Lake, 1913.

his house to settle the dispute with boxing gloves. They would roll back the carpet and get a pail of water and sponges, just as they had seen at the YMCA. Ernest's sister Madelaine usually acted as timekeeper for the bouts. Later, Ernest took boxing lessons in Chicago to improve his skill.

He was a good student at school from the first grade on, and though he started slowly as a reader, he quickly became passionately interested in books and magazines. Throughout his boyhood, Ernest spent hours at a time totally absorbed in reading—sometimes to the point of missing outdoor activities.

Ernest was one of the editors of Oak Park High School's student newspaper and submitted material that was published in the school yearbook. He also wrote some fiction based on Indian stories he had heard in Michigan, although they weren't published at the time. He began to show a natural talent and a desire to write.

By the time Ernest was graduated from high school in 1917, the United States was involved in the First World War. Germany and Austria were battling France, Great Britain, Italy, Russia, and several other countries. German submarines had sunk American ships in the Atlantic, and this and other provocations had resulted in war being declared. Woodrow Wilson was President, and the government in Washington was building up large armed forces and sending troops to fight the powerful German army in France.

It was in this unsettled world that Ernest Hemingway emerged from his sheltered school years—full of vitality and yearning to experience whatever that world had to offer.

Fishing was a favorite pastime of the Hemingway family at their cottage at Walloon Lake. This photograph shows Ernest at age fifteen with some fish he had just caught.

Action was the Goal

To young Ernest Hemingway, who needed to live an active life and was fascinated with guns and the outdoors, joining the armed forces seemed a romantic and desirable idea. No sooner had he graduated from high school than he began asking his parents for permission to enlist.

"I've *got* to get over there and be in some action, before this war ends!" he insisted.

But his parents refused permission. His father, a mild-mannered person who abhorred fighting and violence, was upset to think that his son should want to go to war. Both parents tried to persuade him to enroll in college, but Ernest insisted that he had no interest in a college education. His sister Marcelline, who had graduated with him, was already registered at Oberlin College as a music major, but nobody in the family could convince Ernest that he, too, should go to college. The boy was interested in writing, and

wanted to make his career in that field, and he didn't believe that a college education was necessary for that.

The problem was finally solved when Alfred Tyler Hemingway, an uncle who lived in Kansas City, Missouri, arranged a job for him there. A close friend of Ernest's uncle, an editor on the city's leading newspaper, the Kansas City *Star*, agreed to give Ernest a reporter's job. Ernest was elated and his parents were relieved that he would be near someone in the family.

The Kansas City *Star* was an excellent newspaper, and Ernest was fortunate in being able to associate with top writers and editors in the journalism field. As a cub reporter he was put to work covering fires, fights, accidents, and funerals—the police and hospital beats. He saw the experienced professionals on the city desk rewrite his copy into lean, clear prose that didn't waste words. He was impressed, and he learned.

Top, Ernest and Marcelline on their graduation day from Oak Park (Illinois) High School, 1917. Bottom, Ernest (right) works with Warren Sumner on the Hemingway farm at Walloon Lake while waiting for word on a job with the Kansas City Star, *also in 1917.*

After staying with his aunt and uncle for awhile, Ernest moved downtown into a room of his own. He loved the feeling of independence, and he didn't object to the small salary he was drawing as a beginning reporter. But even this exciting new life couldn't stifle his desire to "see action at the front," and he continued to try to persuade his parents to let him enlist, mentioning it in many of his letters home.

Seeing Ernest out on his own apparently helped his family realize that he should be treated as an adult, and after a few months his father gave him permission to enlist. Ernest, however, had very poor vision in one eye, and none of the armed services would take him. He was dejected, and longed more than ever to get into the war.

Then fate stepped in during a routine newspaper assignment. Ernest was interviewing a group of Italian Red Cross officers who were visiting the United States to recruit volunteers. The Red Cross needed drivers for the ambulance corps on the Italian front, and they were seeking men who were not eligible for the American armed forces, but who were in generally good health.

When he heard that they would accept him even with one bad eye, Ernest immediately signed up. Overjoyed, he wrote excited letters home to his relatives, telling them the news. They were secretly relieved that though he would be at the front, he wouldn't have combat status.

One of his friends from the *Star* had signed up with him, and after one last sojourn of fishing in Michigan, the two young men arrived in New York for passage to Europe. They sailed the last week in May, 1918, aboard a French ship, and after a two-day visit in Paris, arrived in Milan, Italy, in June.

Ernest was put to work driving an ambulance far from the front lines. Since there was not much activity, he quickly became bored with the routine. If only he could get to the front lines, where the action was! He wanted to experience the war firsthand.

Ernest worked with the Italian Red Cross during World War I. Above, Ernest drives an ambulance far from the front lines as his first assignment. Right, Ernest in uniform, at Milan, Italy, in 1918.

Finally he saw his opportunity. There was a special Red Cross volunteer group called the Rolling Canteen Service, which served troops right at the front. The men in the volunteer group rode bicycles to distribute cigarettes and chocolate to the Italian soldiers who were engaged in fighting the Austrian army in northern Italy.

Ernest volunteered for duty with this unit and was soon making his way through the trenches in the Piave sector, where the fighting was heavy. He found all the action he had hoped for. The Austrians constantly shelled the Italian lines with mortars, but the Italians withstood the artillery attack and continued to advance slowly, day by day. Ernest made friends with many of the troops, and they looked forward with pleasure to the young American's visits to the trenches.

In the pre-dawn darkness of July 8, 1918, Ernest was at the front talking with a soldier and beginning his day's activity of distributing cigarettes and chocolate. Suddenly a mortar shell came whistling in and struck only a few yards away. The tremendous blast killed one man, blew the legs off another, and threw Ernest onto the ground, knocking him unconscious. When he came to, Ernest was bleeding and realized he had been hit in the legs with shrapnel.

Spotting a badly wounded soldier near him, Ernest picked him up bodily and began carrying him toward the rear lines for medical attention. As he stumbled along in the mud he was hit in the leg twice by machine gun bullets, but he kept going. Though he felt weak from his wounds, he did not put the other man down until he finally reached

---

Ernest is hit in the legs by more than two hundred pieces of shrapnel from an enemy mortar shell during the course of his duties in the Rolling Canteen Service.

a first-aid station. Then he fainted. So much of the wounded soldier's blood had covered Ernest's coat that the medics at first thought Ernest was wounded in the chest, too.

He was taken to a hospital, where it was discovered that he had more than two hundred pieces of shrapnel in his legs, besides damage from the machine gun bullets. Operations and treatment required more than three months.

Ernest's Red Cross buddies wrote to his parents describing the incident, and his father sent the letters to the local newspaper, which printed them. An Italian officer who had witnessed Ernest's brave action recommended him for a medal of valor, and he was soon decorated by the Italian government. This, too, was reported by the Oak Park newspaper and Ernest immediately became the local war hero. The stories became more and more exaggerated. Some even reported that Er-

Ernest met an American nurse while he was in the hospital in Italy having surgery to remove the shrapnel from his legs. She was his first love, and she became the model for Catherine Barkley, the heroine of A Farewell to Arms.

nest had been made a lieutenant in the Italian army and had fought in combat, which was untrue.

It was during his three months of convalescence in the hospital that Ernest experienced his first true love. A young, pretty American nurse named Agnes von Kurowsky worked on his ward. She and Ernest were quickly attracted to each other. Ernest was a handsome young man, well-built, with a ready wit and a cheerful smile. She was a graceful, poised young woman who was a little older than he. They talked for hours at night, during the day, and any time they could be alone together. Their attraction soon blossomed into love, and they couldn't bear to be apart.

Agnes was transferred to another hospital, however, and they had to keep in contact through letters. Ernest visited her at her place of work after his release and they took long walks in the woods, drank wine in little cafés, and attended the races. Ernest finally proposed marriage to her, but she turned him down, reasoning that he was immature and might later regret his act. He was crushed and bitter, but he eventually got over it.

Agnes had no way of knowing it at the time, but she was to serve as the model for one of Ernest Hemingway's most famous heroines, Catherine Barkley in *A Farewell to Arms*. Ernest wrote to her years later, telling her of a return visit to Italy he had made, and how it stirred memories of her.

In November, 1918, Germany and Austria realized they were defeated and signed an armistice, ending the First World War. Ernest went home, leaving a vital experience behind him —one that helped shape his character and was to provide him with material for some of the great writing he was later to do.

GATHERING IN HONOR OF
LIEUT. ERNEST HENINGWAY
FEB. 16, 1919

Ambition and Pain

It was an excited Hemingway family that welcomed Ernest home from the war. Friends and neighbors gathered at the house in great numbers; the local newspaper interviewed him about his war experiences and wrote a glowing account of his bravery, and he was asked to speak at meetings of various Oak Park organizations. Everyone paid him the respect due a war hero.

Ernest enjoyed all of this hugely, and played the role to the hilt, even though his eyes took on a mischievous twinkle and he could hardly keep from laughing at the exaggerated accounts of his war experiences. He still limped and used a cane, and he often wore an Italian military uniform, such as the Red Cross workers had worn in Italy. Actually, he was in considerable pain, for the many small shrapnel wounds continued to fester for a long time.

He spent his first summer after the war at Walloon Lake, where he hiked through the beautiful Michigan woods again and fished with some of his boyhood pals. His parents had hoped that the maturing experience of wartime danger had changed Ernest—that now he would see the wisdom of going to college. But he was more convinced than ever that he wanted to be a writer, and college still had no place in his life.

Ernest wrote short stories and articles throughout that summer and fall. Though he submitted them to many different magazines, they all came back with rejection slips. He still hadn't learned the professional skill necessary to sell his material to magazines, but he continued to try. He would rush to the mailbox each day, and his hopes would rise for a moment whenever he saw an envelope from a publishing company. Tearing it open, his eyes would fall on the familiar slip of printed paper that informed him impersonally that they had no use for his manuscript. Even more discouraging was the fact that his parents didn't consider his writing efforts "work," and wondered why he was loafing instead of going out and finding a job. He had no acceptable answer, for he hadn't earned a penny from his writing.

His first break came in the winter of 1919 when a family friend who lived in Toronto, Canada, offered Ernest a job tutoring the man's young son. He could live with the family, and would be introduced to one of the editors of the Toronto *Star*, who might be interested in having him do some writing. Ernest jumped at the chance, and shortly after arriving in Toronto he met the editor and arranged to submit material to the paper on a free-lance basis. He wouldn't be a full-time employee, but the paper would use some of his articles and pay him a standard rate for each one they bought. Ernest managed to sell fifteen articles during

---

An "Italian party" in the music room of the Hemingway home in Oak Park, celebrating Ernest's return from World War I. Ernest is pictured in the center, under the Italian flag.

that winter and spring, and seeing his name in print restored his faith in himself as a writer. It was only newspaper writing and he still hadn't sold anything to magazines, but his hopes were buoyed.

Ernest returned to Michigan again for the summer of 1920, where he stayed part of the time with friends who lived near the Hemingways' cottage, rather than with his family. He was restless and moody that summer, not sure what he wanted to do next, and his parents began to lose patience with his listlessness. They had been raised in a generation when a young man was supposed to get a job or go to school, not loaf. Ernest not only loafed that summer, but was reluctant to help with chores around the family cottage and disliked taking direction from his parents. He had undergone experiences and seen parts of the world that most of his relatives and friends knew nothing about, and felt that he was no longer a child. His parents resented this unwillingness to pay attention to what they called "family duty."

A clash was inevitable, and it came. On Ernest's twenty-first birthday his mother presented him with a letter informing him that he would not be welcome in the Hemingway home until he went to work, accepted some responsibility, and began to act like an adult. Dr. Hemingway, who was back in Chicago at the time attending to his medical practice, had agreed with her that this drastic step was necessary.

Both parents hoped that this would shock Ernest out of his growing laziness and lack of concern for his family's feelings. It didn't seem to matter to Ernest that his loafing bothered his parents. Actually, the letter hurt him and made him indignant, and he resolved that he would make his own way in the world

Here Ernest is shown fishing, his major pastime during the summer of 1920. His parents thought he should be more attentive to "family duty."

without his parents' help. In this respect the letter did what his parents had hoped it would do, but the harshness of it left a gulf between them and their son. Yet it was this clash that gave Ernest the independence he needed to make his own career in the world. He no longer felt obligated to worry about fitting into the family's life in Oak Park. It also gave him the necessary motivation to prove himself as a writer.

When the family moved back to Oak Park that fall, Ernest stopped there only long enough to collect his belongings. He then moved in with friends who lived in a Chicago apartment.

One of the friends knew Sherwood Anderson, who was a successful author. Ernest was delighted to meet him and tell him of his literary ambitions.

The Hemingway family's stinging criticism of Ernest's lack of ambition had its effect, and the young man promptly landed a writing job on a small magazine called *Cooperative Commonwealth*. He then was able to face his parents—he was employed and had his own place in which to live.

While he was living in the Chicago apartment, Ernest met and fell in love with a lovely girl named Hadley Richardson. The two had been attracted to each other instantly, and this cultured girl, who had studied music for years, believed in Ernest's ability as a writer. They were married the following summer, but only after Ernest had made it clear that he did not expect to settle down in the comfortable social life of Oak Park. He wanted to travel; maybe go to Europe to write for a living. He also pointed out that he didn't want a big wedding that would involve everybody his family and her family knew. Hadley felt the same way Ernest did about nearly everything and the two were enthusiastic about the future.

The elder Hemingways approved of Hadley, and they were happy to go along with the couple's request for a simple wedding in Michigan and the use of the family cottage for a honeymoon. A number of family friends and relatives did attend the ceremony, and it was a large wedding for the little white Methodist church in Horton's Bay. The wedding took place on a beautiful September day in 1921. The leaves on the elm trees had not yet changed color and the warm summer sun still shone through the church's stained-glass windows. The bride looked radiant and Ernest looked like a typically nervous groom. The elder Hemingways were proud and happy, for they believed that marriage to a good woman might mature their son and help him to ease back into the Oak Park social life and settle down.

Ernest, however, had his own plans. He and the new Mrs. Hemingway moved into a small apartment in Chicago that fall. His enthusiasm for Europe grew even greater when Sherwood Anderson, who had recently returned from there, told him about the literary scene in Paris. A number of young writers had moved there, and they were free to write the way they wanted to, without the pressures of hometown society.

Ernest was convinced now that he must go to Europe to try to establish himself as a writer. He and Hadley packed up and went to Toronto, where he tried to get a salaried job as European correspondent for the *Star*. There was no salaried job available, but the *Star* needed stories from Europe and agreed to pay him for each one of his that they published, as well as his expenses in getting the story. This was good enough for Ernest. He was sure that he and Hadley would be able to get by with the small amount of money

he had saved, if he began to sell stories soon after he arrived there.

Sherwood Anderson had given Ernest letters of introduction to literary people in Paris, and he felt certain that he would be able to establish himself with the right people there and eventually find a market for his writing. In the meantime, he could sell his material to the *Star* and live cheaply. It was easy to live inexpensively in Paris in the 1920's if one didn't crave luxuries, and the only luxury Ernest Hemingway craved was the opportunity to devote himself completely to the task of becoming a successful writer.

Down through history there have been several periods when Paris was the literary and artistic center of the world. It has always been a favorite place for young artists, writers, and musicians. Traditionally, they have been accepted in this city, rather than misunderstood because they are "different." During the 1920's, a large number of talented young writers and artists flocked to Paris and went on to fame. Europe, having recovered from the horror of the First World War, was prosperous. People seemed intent on having a good time, and Paris was one of the liveliest of European cities.

The wedding of Ernest Hemingway and Hadley Richardson in September, 1921, at Horton's Bay, Michigan. Left to right: Ursula, Hadley, Ernest, Mrs. Hemingway, Leicester, and Dr. Hemingway.

The Making of a Writer

The high-spirited young Hemingways had a delightful ocean crossing on their way to a new life in Paris. They traveled aboard an old liner, the *Leopoldina*, and became two of the most popular passengers. Hadley, who had studied piano for years, entertained almost every evening, to the delight of the other passengers and crew. Ernest met a professional boxer and engaged in several bouts with him. The boxer praised Ernest's ability and even suggested that he consider turning professional. Ernest didn't take his advice, but he did retain a strong interest in boxing for the rest of his life.

The Hemingways were quickly settled in a small apartment. Ernest, who found he was able to keep busy as a newspaper correspondent, traveled to Germany, Italy, Switzerland, Greece, and Turkey covering various events, often taking Hadley with him. He interviewed great statesmen, military leaders, and prominent literary figures. The editors of the Toronto *Star* liked his vivid stories and he had no trouble selling them. In a short while he was promoted to a full-salary foreign correspondent, which helped ease his financial burden.

The letters of introduction from Sherwood Anderson proved useful, too. Ernest quickly became a good friend of Sylvia Beach, who operated a bookstore called Shakespeare and Company. The bookstore was a gathering place for several American and English writers who were trying to establish themselves in the literary world. Sylvia Beach was quite well known in the literary community in Paris, and through her Ernest was able to meet many successful and not-so-successful writers. The American poet Ezra Pound befriended Ernest and encouraged him, as did Gertrude Stein, an older woman who was an accepted

Ernest and Hadley are shown walking down a street in Paris. They enjoyed their life in that city, and they were often able to travel through Europe when Ernest had to cover stories for the Toronto Star.

writer. He visited her often, and she gave him much advice, criticized his writing, and urged him to write more. She was impressed with Ernest's talent, though it was undeveloped, and praised him to other influential literary people. James Joyce and Archibald MacLeish also were in his circle of friends, and he received encouragement from them.

Though Ernest's newspaper assignments kept him busy, he continued to write short stories in his spare time. He tried to remember exactly the way the state of Michigan had felt, smelled, and looked to him, and attempted to capture this on paper. Most of the stories he wrote were about a young man like himself, to whom he gave the name Nick Adams. Taking the advice of older writers, he wrote mostly about people and places that were familiar to him. He described the fishing and hunting that was done in Michigan and wrote about the people who vacationed there each year. He devised his own plots, but wove into them characters and events that he remembered well and could describe realistically. He wrote in brisk, clear sentences, a style that had been shaped in great part by his newspaper training. In spite of Gertrude Stein's opinion that Ernest's stories were excellent, however, he hadn't been able to get them published. He also wrote some poems, but they didn't sell either.

While in Paris, Ernest eventually met an American named Robert McAlmon, who owned a small printing press. McAlmon had published a book of poetry by Ezra Pound, and liked Ernest's short stories and poems enough to print a collection of them as a book titled *Three Stories and Ten Poems*. The book, though it was not a big seller (only 300 copies were published), did help Ernest to become better known among literary and publishing people in Europe. Today, the book is a collector's item.

At this time, late in 1923, the Ernest Hemingways were expecting their first child to be born, and they decided to return to Toronto. Ernest went to work in the city room of the *Star* as a correspondent, where he continued to interview and write about celebrities. He had become fascinated with bullfighting during a visit to Spain and wrote two vivid articles on the subject for the paper's weekly magazine. These were well received by the Canadian readers.

The Hemingways' first son, John Hadley Nicanor Hemingway, was born that fall. Ernest's parents were overjoyed with both the family addition and the fact that Ernest was settling down to a more conventional job in North America. But Ernest didn't get along with the editor who was his immediate superior at the *Star,* and he was unhappy in Toronto. He felt also that he shouldn't continue to work in the newspaper field if he wanted to succeed as an author. After an argument with the editor, he quit the paper and decided to return to Europe with Hadley and the baby. The time had come to prove to himself that he could make his way in the world as a writer. It would be a difficult road ahead, but he reasoned that if he didn't take the risk now, he might never have another opportunity.

After a brief visit with his parents, Ernest packed up his small family and went back to Europe. Their friends in Paris were glad to see the Hemingways again and they were soon settled in a low-rent apartment. The baby, whom they nicknamed "Bumby," was a happy, healthy child.

The Hemingways hadn't been in Paris long when Ernest met Ford Madox Ford, a well-known writer and editor of a literary magazine called the *Transatlantic Review.* Ford liked Ernest and was immediately impressed with his short stories, some of which he published in the magazine. Ernest began working as an unpaid associate editor of the magazine so that he would have the opportunity to learn more about what editors wanted. His editorial position also made it possible for him to help get some of Gertrude Stein's work published.

Ernest continued to submit his own stories to well-known magazines, but they still came back with rejection slips. It was such a disheartening experience to pour his soul into a story and then see it come back with an impersonal rejection slip that he sometimes wept. But he never stopped trying, and continued to learn as much as possible about writing and publishing.

He loved the camaraderie of the writers in Paris, for they had many good times together in spite of their relative poverty. They talked for hours over inexpensive wine in small cafés, stimulating each other with their ideas. They packed bread, cheese, and wine and went bicycling through the French countryside. They stayed up all night in each other's apartments, talking, singing, reminiscing about their hometowns and planning their futures.

The matador and the bull in the ring at Pamplona, Spain. Bullfighting was a favorite spectator sport for Ernest, and his book The Sun Also Rises *was set in this background.*

Though Ernest Hemingway often became discouraged and was often short of money during his days as a struggling writer, he refused to change his style of writing to fit the popular magazines of the 1920's. He continued to write the type of story he sincerely believed in, and when his efforts were returned by editors with rejection slips enclosed, he saved them for the day when they would be accepted.

Hemingway was covering the Lausanne Conference for the Toronto Star in 1923 just prior to Christmas when he asked his wife, Hadley, to take a train from Paris and join him. Rather than leave his collection of stories in Paris, Hadley packed them all into a suitcase and brought it with her. The suitcase contained all the stories he had ever written, both originals and carbon copies, plus the first draft of a novel.

Hadley kept the suitcase in her compartment while she was en route. At one point, she left the compartment for a moment to get a drink of water. When she came back the bag was gone. A thief had snatched it, and since the train was in a station at the time, he had made a clean getaway.

Sick at heart, the Hemingways tried everything they could think of to recover the suitcase, but it was never found. The thief had no way of knowing how valuable these manuscripts would someday be, and he probably threw them away in disgust. Ernest had to write every one of the stories over again from memory, as best he could. The loss was a misfortune that he never quite got over.

It was during this period that Ernest met F. Scott Fitzgerald, a young American writer who had already become a success in the United States. Fitzgerald's writing was being hailed as the finest to have appeared in years. He was to go on to a prominent place among American writers of this century with such books as *The Great Gatsby* and *Tender is the Night*. He and Ernest became close friends and spent many happy hours in cafés, drinking Cognac and telling stories to each other.

Fitzgerald was a generous person and rather than feeling a jealous rivalry with Ernest, whose writing he knew to be good, he praised his ability to everyone he knew. Fitzgerald was so impressed with Ernest's writing that he recommended him to the editors at Scribner's, a top American publishing firm where Fitzgerald himself was already solidly established. But they did not accept any of Ernest's work at that time.

Another writer friend of Ernest's who was destined to occupy a prominent place in the literary world was John Dos Passos, also an American. Dos Passos, Ernest, and another writer named Donald Ogden Stewart went to Spain in the summer of 1924 to attend the famous Pamplona fiesta. They joined in the old custom of running before a herd of bulls that is released in the street at the beginning of the bullfight season. One bull caught up with Stewart and Ernest, and bruised them quite severely. *The Sun Also Rises*, Ernest's first serious novel, came partially out of this visit to Spain.

The townspeople of Pamplona run before the bulls through the streets of the town. This is a traditional feature of the annual fiesta in Pamplona, and immediately precedes the bullfighting season. Ernest was severely bruised by one of the bulls at the fiesta in 1925.

45

In the winter Ernest took Hadley and the baby to the Alps, where they found inexpensive accommodations and skied for several weeks. He loved the mountain snow country, and while he was there spent some of his time writing.

Through Bill Bird, another American who owned a small printing press, Ernest arranged to have a second book published. This one was a collection of short stories titled *In Our Time*; again only a small number of copies were printed. The book included many of the short stories Ernest had written about Michigan, stories that foreshadowed the Hemingway style that was to become famous. His great literary goal was realism. He strove to show people as they really are, rather than an idealized picture of what they should be. He wrote with a swift-paced style, never wasting a word in his clear, unemotional prose.

More critics saw copies of this book than had seen his other work. They admired the writing and gave him good reviews in several important magazines. After these reviews appeared, a larger publishing company agreed to publish *In Our Time*, and at last Ernest began to get some recognition.

Shortly afterward, his parents received an order form for the new book from the little publishing company in Paris. They ordered a half dozen copies and anxiously awaited their arrival. When the books arrived, however, they were greatly shocked at the stories. To their Victorian way of thinking, a gentleman should not write about un-

Ernest and Hadley skiing in the Alps in the winter of 1925. Skiing was another sport which Ernest greatly enjoyed, and he and his family could easily find inexpensive accommodations in the Alps for their vacation.

pleasant things or bad moral behavior. They recognized some of the characters in the stories as Michigan people they had known for a long time. The characters were portrayed as bad people with many faults, involved in sordid situations. The elder Hemingways couldn't understand how their son, with his good upbringing, could write this way about people. In fact, they were so shocked and indignant that Dr. Hemingway packed the books back into the box and returned them to the publishing company.

Ernest was hurt and resentful when he found out that his own parents didn't appreciate his writing—especially at a time when some leading critics were discovering that he was an exceptionally gifted writer. More than anything else he wanted his parents to be impressed with his ability, and he was crushed when they didn't judge it fairly.

He stopped writing home for quite awhile, although Hadley continued to correspond with the family. A little later, when some of his stories were published in leading magazines, his father wrote that he would like to see more of his work, since the stories he has seen were about subjects more to his liking than the ones in *In Our Time*.

Ernest wrote back, saying he had thought his parents were not interested in seeing his work, since they had returned the copies of *In Our Time*. Then he went on to explain why he wrote as he did. He pointed out that he wanted to portray life as it really is, and he wanted the reader to be able to feel that these stories were real life. To do this, he said, it was necessary to show the ugly part of life as well as the beautiful. He wanted to show all sides of life, not just the bad side and not just the good side. He added that he hoped they would judge his writing as a whole, rather than on the basis of one story they didn't happen to like.

After the success of *In Our Time*, F. Scott Fitzgerald was able to persuade Scribner's to take on Ernest as an author when his next book was ready. As it turned out, he had two books ready the next year. The shorter one was a satire called *The Torrents of Spring* and the longer one was the first serious novel he had written—*The Sun Also Rises*. He had worked on the novel, based on people he had known in Europe, through much of 1925.

The Sun Also Rises became a best seller on two continents when it was published in 1926. At last Ernest Hemingway from Oak Park, Illinois, was a famous author. Since both the critics and the public liked the book, Ernest felt that his parents would at least have to take note of his success even if they themselves didn't like the book. The elder Hemingways, again judging the book in the light of their own sheltered lives, were thoroughly aghast at the wild lives and immoral behavior of the people portrayed in it. They wrote him that they disliked the novel and couldn't understand why he had written it. Their attitude toward his writing was just what it had been before. Ernest again defended his choice of subject, stressing once more his goal of writing realistically. He could write only what he felt was honest and truthful, and said he would starve rather than write any other way.

Hemingway had indeed struggled hard for a considerable period of time before the public finally accepted his style of writing. Now, at a time when he had finally achieved his goal, there were other problems in his life. He and Hadley had been having difficulty getting along together, and they finally decided to obtain a divorce. They went through with it very quickly, but Ernest hesitated to tell his parents. When he finally informed them, they were very angry and bitterly disappointed in him. They were ashamed and humiliated, for there hadn't been a divorce in the family for generations. But they continued to write to Ernest, and he, in turn, replied to them.

That same year, 1927, Ernest married Pauline Pfeiffer, whom he had known for some time in Europe. She was a charming, even-tempered, adaptable young lady who quickly felt at home in her new husband's unpredictable, non-routine life.

In the fall of 1927 Hemingway was hard at work on a new book, a collection of short stories called *Men Without Women*, which was to be published the following year. One of the stories, *The Killers*, was set in a small diner that Ernest remembered from the days he was living in Chicago with friends. This was to become known as one of his most famous short stories, and was later adapted for movies and television. A British critic wrote in 1928 that there was no finer storywriter in England or America than the author of *The Killers*. Not many American critics disagreed.

Ernest Hemingway had made his mark at last, and he decided it was time to come home to the United States. He and Pauline sailed for home in 1928. Ernest had a record of solid achievement behind him and greater goals ahead of him.

Hemingway returned to the United States in 1928 as a literary hero with a solidly established reputation as one of the best modern writers. Here his ship is shown docking in New York Harbor.

Sunshine and Sweet Success

Ernest Hemingway's struggle for literary acceptance and recognition was won by the time he returned to the United States in 1928. He continued to work hard, however, beginning another full-scale novel at about this time.

Pauline was expecting a child and Ernest wanted to find a place where she could rest and enjoy warm sunshine. The warmest place he could think of that winter was Florida, and as long as they were heading there, Ernest decided that they might as well go as far south as possible. They bought a yellow Model A Ford coupe and drove all the way to Key West from New York. At that time Key West was the southernmost town in the United States.

Drowsy, peaceful Key West was just what the Hemingways wanted. The sparkling blue water and green subtropical scenery were colorful under the warm Caribbean sun. There were no friends there to interrupt Ernest's writing and he could fish whenever he wanted to relax for a few hours.

Ernest invited his parents down for a visit, for he hadn't seen them in a long time and wanted them to meet Pauline. His father couldn't resist the offer to go fishing and the elder Hemingways caught a train down from Chicago soon afterward. It was a good reunion and everyone was happy to have the opportunity to renew family bonds. Her new in-laws liked Pauline immediately.

Meanwhile, Ernest was working furiously on his new novel, determined to finish it that year. When Pauline expressed a desire to visit her parents in Piggott, Arkansas, Ernest was agreeable—but he packed his typewriter along with their other luggage and continued to write during their visit there. Having decided to stay near her family for the baby's arrival, they went to the nearest major city, Kansas City, where Ernest looked up old friends. A healthy boy whom they named Patrick was born to them in June. Ernest worked on his book continuously during this

The photograph shows Ernest Hemingway when he was at the height of his success, just before he left for Spain to cover the Spanish Civil War. He had written a number of novels, all of which had great popular acceptance.

period, pausing only long enough to do some quail hunting with his in-laws after the young Hemingways had returned to Arkansas.

Finally they returned to their home in Key West, where Ernest began the difficult task of rewriting the book. Other writers might have been satisfied with the first draft of a story they knew was good, but not Ernest. He was painstaking in his quest for perfection. He pored over every page, striving to make every word and sentence just right. Hemingway often said that good books were not written, they were rewritten; his own fine craftsmanship was the result of hard work.

At about this time Ernest's father began to worry constantly, for he had met with some severe losses in stock investments during the previous year. His health was bad and he suffered from diabetes, but he kept his fears to himself. When the cold, gray days of late autumn set in, Dr. Hemingway plunged deeper and deeper into mental depression. It soon became apparent to members of the family that he wasn't himself, but they expected him to pass through this state of depression. On December 6, 1928, however, Dr. Hemingway went to his bedroom, closed the door, and shot himself in the head with a revolver. His suicide shocked the entire community of Oak Park and Mrs. Hemingway had to be placed under sedation.

Ernest received a telegram of notification while on a train from New York to Florida with his oldest son, five-year-old Bumby. The child had just arrived from Europe with his mother, and Ernest was taking him on a visit to Key West. When the telegram arrived, Ernest made arrangements to leave Bumby under a porter's care until the train arrived in Florida. Ernest got off at the next station and caught a train to Chicago. As the oldest son, he took charge of the funeral arrangements and helped the other members of his family in every way possible. He hid his own grief, but it cut him deeply, for he had never stopped loving his father in spite of their disagreements.

A saddened Ernest returned to Key West, where he engaged his sister Madelaine to type the finished manuscript of his book. She was the first person to read it, and knew immediately that he had written a great story. It was based on his war experiences in Italy, with wonderful descriptions of people and the way they react in war. The full horror of war was revealed in vividly created scenes, for Ernest had intended to bring out the senselessness of war and its often disastrous effects

on people. At the same time, it was a haunting love story, based on his own first love of many years ago when he had been in an Italian hospital. The book, *A Farewell to Arms*, was praised by critics and liked by the general public from the time it was first published in 1929. It became an immediate best seller and a Hollywood film studio bought the rights for a motion picture adaptation.

Few writers have attained the degree of critical and financial success and public recognition at such an early age. Hemingway was only thirty years old, yet he could have relaxed and stopped writing for the rest of his life, for he had already hit the peak of success. He did, in fact, slow down his writing output in the years after the publication of *A Farewell to Arms*, for no longer did he have to strive for public acceptance of his writing style.

The Hemingways were able to live quite comfortably now, and after renting two houses in Key West, Ernest and Pauline finally bought one of their own. They both loved the warm climate, the peaceful little town, and the opportunity to swim and fish every day.

Ernest's zest, vitality, and determination were now directed toward fishing, which had long been his favorite pastime. He soon became one of the best fishermen in the Florida Keys, adept at catching huge tarpon, bonefish, marlin, barracuda, and just about every other type of fish around. He learned much about fishing in these waters from fishing cronies and boat operators he met in local taverns down by the docks. One salty character named Josey Russell took him deep-sea fishing off the shore of Cuba, where the catches were bigger than those in the Keys and the struggles more exciting. Ernest was later to model

Ernest fishing in the Caribbean, during the time that he and Pauline were living in Key West. He soon became one of the best fishermen in the Florida Keys, and often fished off the coast of Cuba, where there were bigger, more challenging fish.

55

Harry Morgan, the hero of his book *To Have and Have Not,* after Russell. Humphrey Bogart played this role in the film version.

In the fall and winter Ernest hunted big game in Wyoming and birds in Arkansas and elsewhere. He became an expert shot, despite the fact that he wore glasses because of his nearsightedness. He loved nothing better than to tramp across open fields behind good bird dogs, a gun slung over his shoulder.

Ernest's third son, Gregory, was born in 1932, the same year that a slim book about bullfighting, *Death in the Afternoon,* made its appearance. It was not a novel, but an explanation of bullfighting, which was one of Ernest's great enthusiasms. He admired the ceremony surrounding the bullfights, but even more, he admired the courage of the matadors and the inherent drama of the bullring.

A generous host, Ernest entertained many people in Key West. There were parties galore, at the Hemingways' house and on the yachts of friends. Maxwell Perkins, Ernest's editor at Scribner's, used to come down to escape the winter weather in New York.

Another of Ernest's good friends was a young man named Arnold Gingrich who was then editor of a fashion magazine in Chicago. He, too, had spent his boyhood in Michigan and the two had much in common, including a love of trout fishing. Gingrich told Ernest of his plans to start a new magazine for men. He didn't have much financial backing, but he believed it could be a big success. It would feature quality writing and be sort of a male counterpart of *Vogue* in its advertising. He asked Ernest if he would be willing to write some articles on fishing and hunting for the magazine, even though he couldn't pay him much. Ernest agreed because he liked Gingrich and believed he had a chance to succeed with the magazine. The magazine, *Esquire,* has gone on to become one of the most prestigious publications in the country.

Ernest wasn't writing as much then as he had, but he had enough material from past years to publish a collection of short stories in 1933—*Winner Take Nothing.*

He felt at this time that he deserved an opportunity to enjoy his favorite diversions for awhile, for he had worked very hard to achieve his present status. Even so, his restlessness began to show again and he began planning a new venture. He wanted to travel, experience new things, and collect material for future writing projects. The place that intrigued him most was Africa, a continent that was to play a prominent part in his life.

"Packing in" (hunting on packhorses) in Wyoming. Ernest Hemingway liked hunting of all kinds, from lion hunts in Africa to expeditions in search of big game in Wyoming to bird hunts in Arkansas.

Adventure in Far Places

In the summer of 1933 Ernest Hemingway embarked on a five month sojourn to hunt big game in Africa. Pauline was able to accompany him because they left their two sons with relatives. Ernest also brought along a fishing and hunting pal from Key West named Charles Thompson. Ernest's enthusiasm ran high for several months before the trip began, and he was engrossed in planning the details. After consulting people with experience in African hunting before completing his list of supplies, he included such things as rifles and ammunition for hunting various game, anti-snakebite serum, warm clothing for cold nights and high altitudes, chemicals for purifying drinking water, and food and supplies that he would be unable to get in Africa.

On the way to Africa, the three visited Spain and Paris where Ernest looked up old friends. When their ship stopped at Port Said, Egypt, en route to East Africa, Ernest ate some food that was to cause him great difficulty during the weeks ahead. He became infected with amoebic dysentery, which didn't show up immediately but caused him to become weaker and weaker as the weeks went by.

Ernest had hired an experienced English guide, Philip Percival, who helped make the safari successful from a hunting standpoint. Both Ernest and Charles Thompson proved to be expert shots in Kenya, with Ernest getting a lion, a rhinoceros, and a Cape buffalo in the first weeks. Ernest's first shot at the buffalo only wounded the animal, who then went into some dense underbrush. When Hemingway went after it, the huge animal suddenly charged him. He coolly fired and dropped the beast when it was only a few feet away. He had dreamed of stalking and killing big African game, and insisted on doing this despite the weakness he felt. He had to interrupt the safari at one point, however, to rest in bed because he was

Ernest is shown here with a Cape buffalo, which he killed on a hunting trip in Kenya. It had hidden in some dense foliage, only to charge him unexpectedly.

too ill to continue. But Hemingway used this uncomfortable experience as material in one of his most famous stories, *The Snows of Kilimanjaro*, later made into a motion picture starring Ava Gardner, Gregory Peck, and Susan Hayward. He also drew on his African experiences when he wrote *The Short Happy Life of Francis Macomber*, which also was made into a movie starring Gregory Peck.

On his return to Key West, Hemingway wrote a book about his African observations called *The Green Hills of Africa*, which was published in 1935. He then set to work on his next novel, *To Have and Have Not*, based on Key West and some of the people he knew there. His big expedition over, he was working hard now, as though to make up for lost time.

Hemingway also ordered a fishing cruiser he had dreamed about for several years. The thirty-eight-foot craft, which he named the *Pilar*, was an exceptionally seaworthy boat. He was proud and pleased with it and enjoyed having friends aboard for fishing trips.

Hemingway never tired of fishing, and day after day spent hours on the water. But his self-discipline was strong and he always spent the morning writing. He would rise at five or six A.M. so that he would have time for a good morning's work and still be able to spend the afternoon enjoying himself with his friends.

"Looking forward to the afternoon's fishing gives me the incentive to work harder at the typewriter," he said. He knew that he would not have been able to enjoy himself during the afternoon if he didn't have a feeling of accomplishment after his morning's work.

He gave another piece of advice to writers who have trouble getting started on their daily stint at the typewriter:

"Never stop your day's writing at the end of a chapter or incident," he said. "Always stop in the middle of something when you're going good. Then it will be easier to pick up again the next day where you left off."

He rarely stopped writing, though he spent weeks at a time away from Key West, fishing in the Bahamas and Cuba.

Hemingway and Pauline are pictured here as they arrive home from their three-month hunting expedition in Africa, 1934.

He usually brought his typewriter with him wherever he went.

By 1936 Hemingway was again becoming restless. This mood reflected the mood of all Europe, and the United States. Most of the countries of the world were in a severe economic depression. Millions of people couldn't find employment and citizens of many countries were dissatisfied with the way things were going and wanted a change. In Italy and Germany civil liberties were lost when the fascist parties, who promised to improve the economic situation, took over the governments. Though Benito Mussolini did improve the efficiency of government services in Italy, he became an absolute ruler, while Adolf Hitler had become the dictator of Germany. Anyone who opposed him was tortured, imprisoned, or executed. Both Hitler and Mussolini were building up large armies and threatening to invade and conquer other European countries.

In Spain another fascist leader, General Franco, led a revolt to throw out the legal government of the king. He received help from Hitler and Mussolini in the form of troops, guns, ammunition, and equipment. Soon Spain was plunged into civil war and battles raged across the whole country.

Hemingway had followed the development of the war in Spain from the time it broke out, and decided he wanted to cover it as a correspondent. Because his reputation as a writer was well established, he found it easy to make arrangements with an American newspaper syndicate and was soon on his way to Spain. In addition to filing dispatches from the centers of action, he arranged to produce a documentary film and write the narration.

Hemingway jokes with newsmen as he boards a ship bound for Spain, where he is to cover the Spanish Civil War for an American newspaper syndicate.

The Spanish Civil War was fiercely fought; whole towns and cities were destroyed during the action. The innocent civilians suffered most because of modern artillery and aerial warfare. It was this touching aspect of the war that impressed Hemingway the most.

Most of his time was spent following the infantry of the government forces as they fought the fascist armies. He was in the thick of the action and was able to file vivid accounts of the war, describing the acrid smell of smoke and spent ammunition, the sight of houses bursting into flame when shells hit, and the crackle of rifle fire. The war raged on for many months.

After he returned to the United States, Hemingway appealed for funds to aid the anti-fascist forces and the victims of the war. He returned three more times to cover the action, ranging over the whole country as he accompanied guerrilla forces as well as regular army groups. He was under bombard-

ment in the cities and shot at when he was with the guerrilla bands in the mountains. While he was with the guerrillas, he gathered the material for another novel.

In the meantime he wrote a play, the only one he had ever tried, called *The Fifth Column*. It did not prove to be very successful. His novel about Key West and the Caribbean, *To Have and Have Not*, was doing quite well in sales by this time, however.

By late 1938 it was obvious that the fascists were going to win the civil war, much to the sorrow of Hemingway and many other anti-fascists. He left Spain just before the final surrender. Things were bad in his own life, too. The long separation from his wife and family had caused problems and the marriage was failing. Pauline moved to New York and later got a divorce.

Hemingway plunged into writing his next novel, based on what he had seen and experienced in Spain. For almost a

A scene from the Spanish Civil War. Hemingway, as a foreign correspondent, saw a great deal of combat and was able to send back excellent accounts of the action. He was in Spain a total of four times during the war.

year and a half he struggled, rewriting whole sections of the book so that it would be just the way he wanted it. He moved to Cuba where he wrote most of the book. He still had the *Pilar* and still loved to fish, but his main project was the book. Some of it was written at Sun Valley, Idaho, where he skied and went bird hunting with actor Gary Cooper.

Hemingway continued to see his sons whenever he could, and often took them hunting and skiing out west as well as taking them fishing in Florida.

By 1940, when the book was published, there was no doubt that it was going to be Ernest Hemingway's biggest success. *For Whom the Bell Tolls* was a powerful story stressing the futility of war and the effect it has on people, much as his earlier book, *A Farewell to Arms,* had done. This one, too, contained a touching and tragic love affair between a young American and a European girl during wartime. Hemingway's lean, unemotional prose

During the 1930's, an idealistic young government employee named Tom Bennett, who was a great admirer of Ernest Hemingway, dreamed about someday meeting his idol. During the civil war in Spain, Bennett came very near to fulfilling that dream.

He had joined a volunteer group of American fighters on the side of the anti-fascists and had been wounded three times. One of those times, he was taken to the same hospital where Hemingway was said to have been a patient. But he arrived just one day after the famed author had left, and suffered more from the blow of learning this than from his wounds.

Bennett left Spain not too long afterward, broke and looking for a way back to the United States. He made his way as far as Paris, and by a great stroke of luck, met Hemingway in a bookstore. To Bennett's amazement, Hemingway took a look at the wounded, poverty-stricken young man and handed him a considerable sum of money.

"Go buy some clothes. You're coming home to the States with us. The ship leaves in two days, and I'll book your passage," Hemingway announced crisply. It was a wonderful, warm, friendly voyage home with Hemingway. A starry-eyed young Tom Bennett arrived in New York with a story that he would tell his friends for years to come.

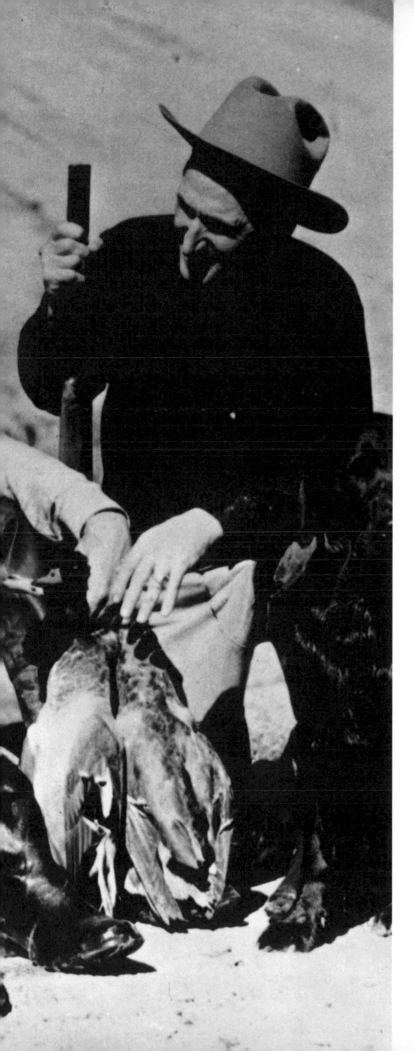

had a powerful simplicity. The book was a masterpiece of writing, and it quickly became the biggest seller Hemingway had ever had.

The film rights were sold to Paramount Studios for $150,000, a record sum for that time. Hemingway felt very strongly about this book, and had sold the film rights with the stipulation that only Ingrid Bergman could play the heroine. He knew she would be perfect for the part. He wanted his friend Gary Cooper to play the male lead role. Cooper agreed, and the film that was made in 1943 was a Hollywood classic. Still shown on television today, it is a perennial favorite.

Hemingway's personal life underwent another change in 1941. He married Martha Gellhorn, an attractive, blond correspondent he had met in Spain during the civil war. They lived outside of Havana, in a house called *Finca Vigia*. It was a handsome old estate on the outskirts of a small fishing village, containing a swimming pool, tennis courts, a rolling lawn, and a tower with a study where he could write. The *Pilar* was anchored in the harbor nearby.

Hemingway seemed to have everything necessary for a peaceful life, but the events to come would be anything but peaceful.

Hemingway on a hunting trip with actor Gary Cooper, a close personal friend, in 1940. Hemingway insisted that Cooper play the male lead in the film version of his book For Whom the Bell Tolls.

World at War

The world had rumbled toward war during the summer of 1939, and Europe was engulfed in conflict when Hitler's armies attacked Poland in September of that year. France and Great Britain had come to the aid of Poland and soon Italy was on the side of Germany. By 1941 the German armies had conquered much of Europe, including France and a large portion of Russia. England was fighting for her life, and American ships carrying supplies to the British were being sunk in the Atlantic by German submarines.

On December 7, 1941, Japanese planes attacked Pearl Harbor in Hawaii, damaging much of the American Pacific fleet. The military leaders who had taken over the government in Japan were bent on conquest in Asia, and the United States stood in their way. Japan hoped to defeat America in a quick campaign, then be free to take Asia. They knew that once industrial leaders such as Henry Ford directed giant production capacities toward the war effort, America would grow more powerful every day.

Hemingway, in Cuba, read the newspapers during the early days of the war. The news was not good. General Douglas MacArthur led an outnumbered force of American and Filipino troops in defense of the Philippines, stalling the Japanese invaders by brilliant strategy. But aid was not available to him, and

Hemingway writing at his typewriter at Sun Valley Lodge, in Idaho. He wrote wherever and whenever he had the opportunity, especially in the days before his fame was established.

it was only a matter of time before the enemy overran the islands and conquered many other places in Asia.

In the Atlantic, the big danger was German submarine activity. Literally hundreds of American ships were sunk while the Nazi submarines roamed at will, sometimes in sight of the American shoreline. The United States Navy was being expanded as fast as men could be recruited and ships built, but this took time. In the meantime, Ernest Hemingway and other boat owners in the Caribbean were on special assignment. They were secretly armed and ordered to cruise as though fishing, keeping a lookout for enemy submarines. If a submarine were to hail them and surface or attack them, they were prepared to shoot at close range with everything they had. The *Pilar*, heavily armed, performed some dangerous reconnaissance missions, but never encountered a submarine.

By 1943, Mrs. Martha Hemingway had gone off to England as a war correspondent, and Ernest decided to do the same thing. He was made chief of the magazine *Collier's* European Bureau in 1944 and covered the preparation for the Allied invasion of France. His brother Leicester was also there in the army as was his oldest son, John, or Bumby, a member of the O.S.S. who was captured and held prisoner by the Germans until the end of the war.

As did most people in wartime London, which was being bombed by German planes. Hemingway attended many impromtu parties and spent a lot of time in pubs. Because no one was certain that he would be alive the next day, people adopted a devil-may-care attitude to forget their worries. Though Hemingway went on some bombing raids over France, his only wound occurred when he was badly cut on the head in an automobile accident.

Ernest Hemingway was one of the few men stationed overseas who was able to see his wife, since Martha was often in London. Their marriage was

London being bombed during a German raid. Both Hemingway and his wife Martha were war correspondents in World War II. The illustration shows Hemingway and a photographer covering one of the German raids.

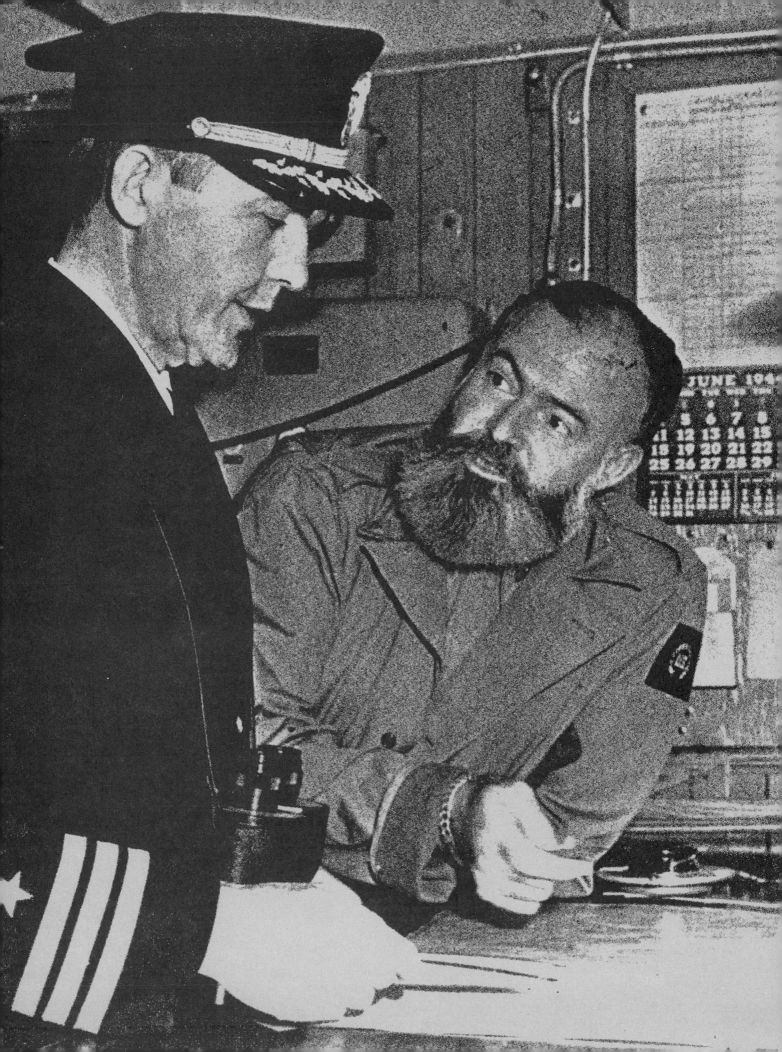

ruined, however, for the strain of war made things difficult and they each had duties to perform that they considered more important than their married life. The marriage ended for all practical purposes and they were divorced in 1945.

Hemingway was one of the combat correspondents in the invasion of France on D-Day, June 6, 1944, and remained in the thick of the action from then on. He was among the first Allied personnel to enter Paris—ahead of most of the army units. From there he accompanied American troops in fierce fighting in Belgium and Germany. He was now wearing a beard because of a skin rash that made shaving painful, and he acquired the nickname "Papa," a name that was to remain with him for the rest of his life.

Having once again evaded bullets and bombs and other dangers, Ernest Hemingway went home at the close of the war in Europe. He had written superb accounts of the fighting in his dispatches, and people wondered if he would write a book about the war. But he never did.

In 1946, Hemingway married Mary Welsh, a correspondent he had met during the war. She was a lively, intelligent girl employed by *Time* magazine who had known Ernest's brother Leicester when they both had worked on a newspaper in Chicago. Her gentle feminine qualities appealed greatly to Ernest, and this marriage was to be the best thing that happened to him.

They settled down at *Finca Vigia*, where Hemingway began the mature period of his life in which he was to produce some of his greatest work.

Far left, Hemingway (left) pores over maps of the French invasion with Navy Commander W. I. Leahy, captain of an attack transport. Left, Hemingway interviews troops at the front.

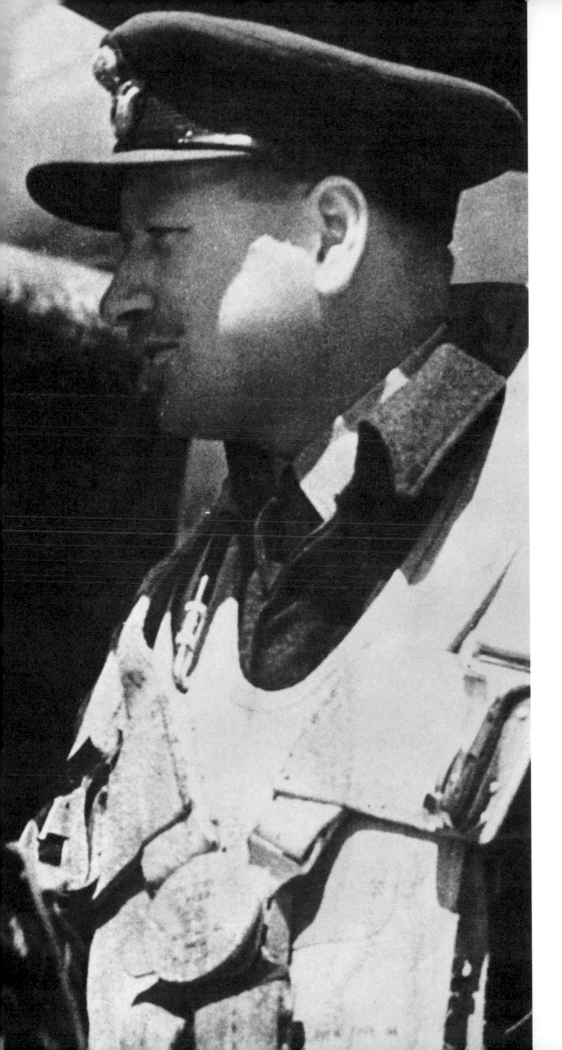

Hemingway (left) talks to his pilot, Wing Commander L. A. Lynn, before taking off from a base in England to accompany a Royal Air Force flight over France.

A Literary Legend

Ernest "Papa" Hemingway became a sort of patriarch of American writers long before he was really old. Celebrities, journalists, and admirers from all walks of life wrote him letters and visited him at his home in Cuba. Millions saw the motion pictures made from his books and stories, and were familiar with the characters and plots of his work. The average American asked during the post-World War II period who the most famous living writer was, would reply unhesitatingly, "Ernest Hemingway, of course."

By this time Hemingway was as much a celebrity himself as any of the movie stars who played roles in the film versions of his books. Newspapers reported his travels, gossip columnists wrote about his fishing exploits, his

fights, and the parties he attended. He was described as a wild, high-spirited adventurer—the stereotype of what many people thought a writer should be.

In truth, he couldn't have created the great literature that he did if he had lived this sort of life constantly. He continued to be a hard worker, never relaxing the same high standards he had always set for himself. At times he was annoyed at the intrusions on his work caused by people calling on him, but he was usually gracious and patient. Mary managed the domestic routine so smoothly and provided him with such warm affection that he was able to turn his energy entirely toward writing.

The house was usually overrun with cats, and the author's faithful dog received much affection. He kept fighting

Top, Hemingway and his fourth wife, the former Mary Welsh, after their wedding in Havana, Cuba, in 1946. Bottom, left to right: Hemingway, Ingrid Bergman, and Charles Boyer at the Stork Club in New York. Miss Bergman played the feminine lead in the movie For Whom the Bell Tolls.

cocks outside and loved to wager on them with men from the local village.

Hemingway's first postwar book, *Across the River and Into the Trees*, was a novel set in Venice, about the love affair of an aging colonel and a young girl. For the first time in his career, a majority of the critics wrote negative opinions of his book. Some said he had written all the great things he was capable of writing and no longer had the dedication he once had. He disagreed vehemently and proved his point a couple of years later by producing what many regard as the finest masterpiece of his career. It was a short book called *The Old Man and the Sea*, published in 1952, first as a serial in *Life* magazine, then as a hard-cover book. It was a beautiful, haunting tale about an old fisherman, his struggle with a huge fish and the elements of nature, and the young boy who believed in him. It was almost Biblical in its simplicity, yet the book moved people with an emotional power seldom encountered in literature.

This time the critics were ecstatic. The book was acclaimed as one of the finest classics of the twentieth century by reviewers of the London *Sunday Times*, the London *Observer*, the New York *Times*, and many other major newspapers. Hemingway was also awarded the Pulitzer Prize for the book. He was grateful and proud, and wished that his parents could have lived to see his triumph. But his mother had died the year before *The Old Man and the Sea* was published, and his father, of course, had died many years earlier.

As his fame grew even greater, Hemingway continued to write and to travel to Europe occasionally. He made his trek to Africa and frightened the world with his two airplane crashes, then spent considerable time recovering in Cuba.

Above, Hemingway enters Paris as a war correspondent—ahead of most of the troops. Right, Hemingway is decorated by the Cuban government for his assistance to them during World War II.

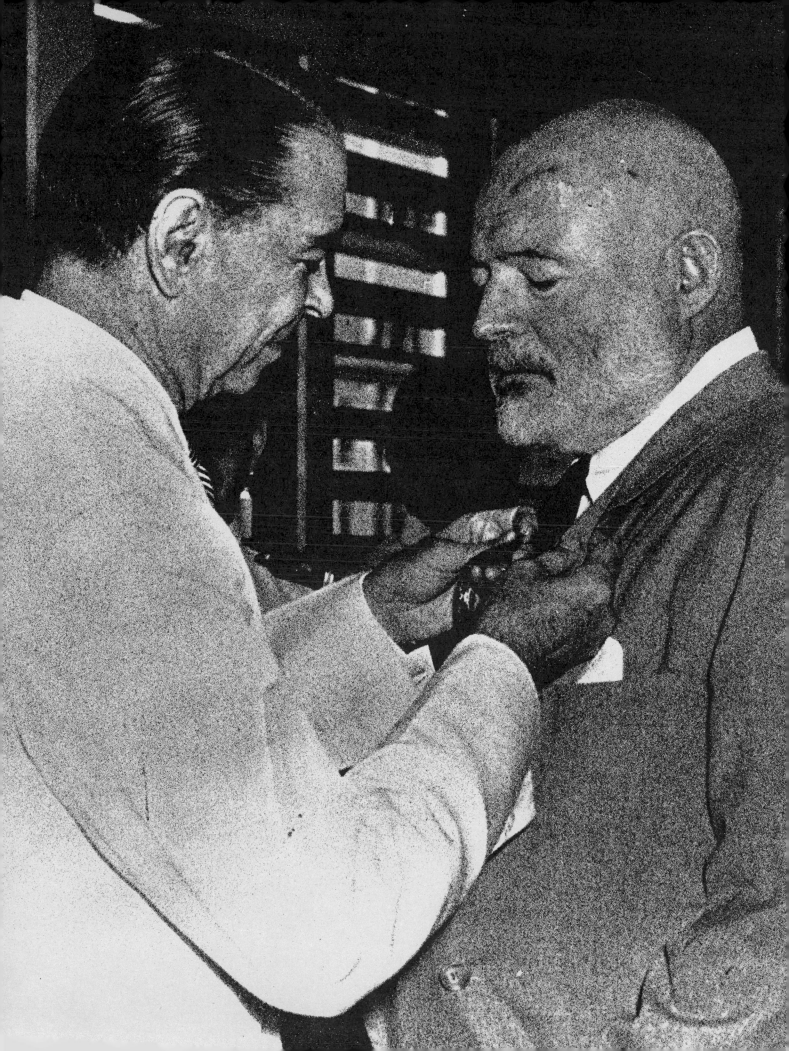

Top left, left to right: Mary Hemingway, Gary Cooper, Mrs. Cooper, and Hemingway at the Stork Club. Bottom left, left to right: Hemingway, Mary, Mrs. Leland Hayward, Spencer Tracy, George Jessel. Right, Hemingway with a marlin caught off the coast of Peru in 1956.

It was during this recovery period that an even greater honor was bestowed upon him: the Nobel Prize for literature, awarded "for his powerful style-forming mastery of the art of modern narration, as most recently evinced in *The Old Man and the Sea* . . ."

Ernest Hemingway had just about run out of worlds to conquer. But he resumed his writing and traveling in the following years, a world-renowned celebrity wherever he went. He returned to Spain for the bullfights and wrote a series of articles on them for *Life* called *The Dangerous Summer*. He took part in the filming of the motion picture version of *The Old Man and the Sea*, piloting the *Pilar* and trying to catch a huge fish for the camera crew. But the fishing was not very good and the studio ended up using a false fish for the scenes with Spencer Tracy as the old fisherman.

Hemingway continued to hunt in the fall near Sun Valley, Idaho, and bought a house nearby in the little town of Ketchum. He and Mary loved the wide, western skies and the grandeur of the Sawtooth Mountains. They kept their home in Cuba and stayed there even after the revolution, led by Fidel Castro, took over the government. But finally, in 1960, he left *Finca Vigia*, destined never to return.

Top right, Hemingway autographing a copy of one of his books. Bottom right, Hemingway (right) talks with Spencer Tracy, star of the film version of his book The Old Man and the Sea.

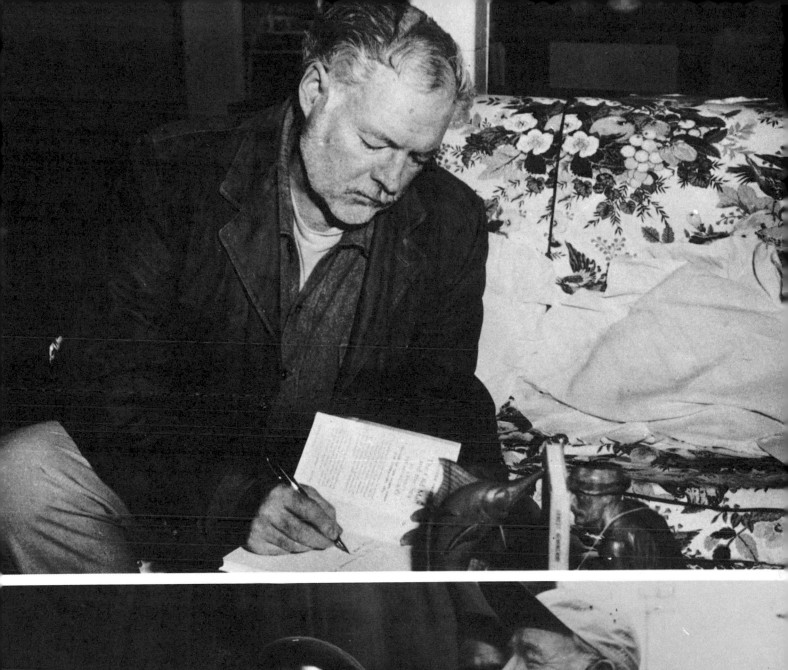

Hemingway's health began to deteriorate during 1960 and he spent considerable time in the famed Mayo Clinic at Rochester, Minnesota. He had always been a rugged man but now he lost weight and his once muscular body became thin and weak. He went home to Idaho between stays at the clinic, but neither his wife's gentle care nor the knowledge of the doctors could restore his health. As the months dragged by he became depressed and a sense of finality seemed to pervade his thoughts. He had lived his life to the fullest, and there seemed nothing left.

Early on the morning of July 2, 1961, Hemingway sat with his favorite shotgun in his house in Ketchum. As the morning sun stole across the high mountains and into the valley, the stillness of the air was shattered by the blast of the gun. Ernest Hemingway had died instantly. He was buried in the small cemetery not far from his house, in the shadow of the Sawtooth Mountains.

He had once written:

"There are some things which cannot be learned quickly, and time, which is all we have, must be paid heavily for their acquiring. They are the very simplest things, and because it takes a man's life to know them the little new that each man gets from life is very costly and the only heritage he has to leave."

Ernest Hemingway left a magnificent heritage in the beauty and wisdom of his writing. It was his destiny to be more important than any other writer of our age.

Friends of Ernest Hemingway carry his casket to its final resting place in the Ketchum, Idaho, cemetery. Most of these men are residents of Ketchum, where Hemingway had lived for the last few years of his life.

Summary

In more than two centuries, few American writers had won the respect and admiration of the learned scholars of European civilization. Where were the great American writers? they asked. Where were the novelists who commanded accolades from a universal readership?

It was the destiny of Ernest Hemingway to break this barrier of acceptance. He was a writer who did not imitate the traditional styles of great literature. With clean, powerful strokes he forged his own style of writing—a natural, realistic style that was refreshingly different from any that had been seen before. He labored to perfect this style with a devotion seldom seen, even among great novelists, and he never compromised his standards for the opportunity to make money. His long, hard, self-imposed apprenticeship made him a master when other writers had stopped trying to improve.

Hemingway had the flair to become a world celebrity and he became the most famous American writer of all time. Because of his popularity, the gift of his writing reached more people than that of any American writer before him, and it ensured a permanent place in history for American literature.

Bibliography

ALDRIDGE, JOHN. *After the Lost Generation.* New York: The Noonday Press, 1958.

ANDERSON, SHERWOOD. *Memoirs.* New York: Harcourt, Brace, 1942.

ARONOWITZ, ALFRED G. and Peter Hamill. *Ernest Hemingway, the Life and Death of a Man.* New York: Lancer, 1961.

BAKER, CARLOS. *Hemingway, The Writer as Artist.* Princeton: Princeton University Press, 1956.

BAKEWELL, CHARLES M. *The Story of the American Red Cross in Italy.* New York: Macmillan, 1920.

BEACH, SYLVIA. *Shakespeare and Company.* New York: Harcourt, Brace, 1956.

BERTON, PIERRE. "Hindmarsh of the Star." *Macleans,* April 1, 1952.

BISHOP, JOHN PEALE. "Homage to Hemingway." *New Republic,* November 11, 1936.

BREIT, HARVEY. "Talk With Ernest Hemingway." *New York Times Book Review,* September 7, 1952.

———. "Talk With Mr. Hemingway." *New York Times Book Review,* September 17, 1950.

BRINNIN, JOHN MALCOLM. *The Third Rose, Gertrude Stein and Her World.* New York: Grove Press, 1959.

BRUMBACK, THEODORE. "With Hemingway Before A Farewell to Arms." *Kansas City Star,* December 6, 1936.

COHEN, LOUIS H. *A Bibliography of the Works of Ernest Hemingway.* New York: 1931.

COWLEY, MALCOLM. *Exile's Return.* New York: Viking Press, 1951.

———. Introduction to *The Viking Portable Hemingway.* New York: Viking Press, 1944.

CRANSTON, HERBERT. *Ink On My Fingers.* New York: Ryerson Press, 1953.

———. "When Hemingway Earned Half a Cent a Word on the Toronto Star." *New York Herald Tribune Book Review,* January 13, 1952.

DURANTY, WALTER. *I Write As I Please.* New York: Simon & Schuster, 1935.

EASTMAN, MAX. *Great Companions.* New York: Farrar, Straus and Cudahy, 1959.

FALLACI, ORIANA. "An Interview with Mary Hemingway." *Look,* September 6, 1966. (Primarily a reply to the controversial Hotchner book.)

FENTON, CHARLES A. *The Apprenticeship of Ernest Hemingway, The Early Years.* New York: Viking Press, 1954.

FIEDLER, LESLIE A. *Love and Death in the American Novel.* New York: Criterion Books, 1960.

GALLUP, DONALD, ed. *The Flowers of Friendship: Letters Written to Gertrude Stein.* New York: Knopf, 1953.

HEMINGWAY, ERNEST. *Three Stories and Ten Poems*. Paris: Contact Publishers, 1923.

————. *In Our Time*. Paris: 1924.

————. *In Our Time*. (enlarged edition) New York: Boni & Liveright, 1925.

————. *The Torrents of Spring*. New York: Scribner's, 1926.

————. *The Sun Also Rises*. New York: Scribner's, 1926.

————. *Men Without Women*. New York: Scribner's, 1927.

————. *A Farewell to Arms*. New York: Scribner's 1929.

————. *Death in the Afternoon*. New York: Scribner's, 1932.

————. *Winner Take Nothing*. New York: Scribner's, 1933.

————. *The Green Hills of Africa*. New York: Scribner's, 1935.

————. *To Have and Have Not*. New York: Scribner's, 1937.

————. *The Fifth Column*. New York: Scribner's, 1938.

————. *The First Forty-Nine Short Stories* (including "The Snows of Kilimanjaro" and "The Short Happy Life of Francis Macomber"). New York: Scribner's, 1938.

————. *For Whom the Bell Tolls*. New York: Scribner's, 1940.

————. *Across the River and Into the Trees*. New York: Scribner's, 1950.

————. *The Old Man and the Sea*. New York: Scribner's, 1952.

————. *A Moveable Feast*. New York: Scribner's, 1964 (posthumous)

————. "A Divine Gesture." *Double-Dealer*, May, 1922. (Hemingway's first serious story to be published, a fable not collected elsewhere.)

————. "They All Want Peace—What Is Peace?" *Little Review*, Spring, 1923.

————. "Homage to Ezra." *This Quarter*, May, 1925.

————. "In Defense of Dirty Words." *Esquire*, September, 1934.

————. "Old Newsman Writes." *Esquire*, December, 1934.

————. "A.D. Southern Style: A Key West Letter." *Esquire*, May, 1935.

————. "Monologue to the Maestro." *Esquire*, October, 1935.

————. "The Malady of Power." *Esquire*, November, 1935.

———— "On Blue Water." *Esquire*, April, 1936.

————. Introduction to *Men At War*. New York: Crown, 1942.

————. "The Faithful Bull." *Holiday*, March, 1951. (a fable)

————. "The Good Lion." *Holiday*, April, 1951. (a fable)

————. "Christmas Gift." *Look*, April 20, 1954 and May 4, 1954.

————. "A Visit With Ernest Hemingway." *Look*, September 4, 1956.

————. "The Dangerous Summer." *Life*, September 5, 1960, September 12, 1960, and September 19, 1960.

————. A number of Hemingway stories have not been collected, including several published in the *Atlantic* in the 1950's. It is said that his wife will publish more stories and a novel within a few years.

HEMINGWAY, LEICESTER. *My Brother, Ernest Hemingway*. New York: World, 1961.

HERBST, JOSEPHINE. "The Starched Blue Sky of Spain." *The Noble Savage*, Spring, 1960.

HOTCHNER, A.E. *Papa Hemingway*. New York: Random House, Inc., 1966.

KILEY, JED. *Hemingway, An Old Friend Remembers*. New York: Hawthorn Books, 1965.

LANIA, LEO. *Hemingway, A Pictorial Biography*. New York: Viking Press, 1961.

LEWIS, WYNDHAM. *Men Without Art*. London: 1934.

LOEB, HAROLD. *The Way It Was*. New York: Criterion Books, 1959.

LUDOVICI, L. J. *Nobel Prize Winners*. Westport, Conn.: Associated Booksellers, 1957.

McCAFFERY, JOHN K. M. *Ernest Hemingway, The Man and His Work*. New York: Avon, 1950 and Cleveland, Ohio: World, 1950. (a collection of important essays on Hemingway)

MACLEISH, ARCHIBALD. "His Mirror Was Danger." *Life*, July 14, 1961.

MIZENER, ARTHUR. *The Far Side of Paradise*. New York: Houghton, Mifflin Company, 1949.

NORMAN, CHARLES. *Erza Pound*. New York: Macmillan, 1960.

PLIMPTON, GEORGE. "The Art of Fiction XXI—Ernest Hemingway." *Paris Review*, Spring, 1958. Also collected in book form with other *Paris Review* interviews.

POORE, CHARLES, ed. *The Hemingway Reader*. New York: Scribner's, 1953. (Reprints of some pieces not in any of the short story collections. There is no complete edition of Hemingway's work.)

PUTNAM, SAMUEL. *Paris Was Our Mistress*. New York: Viking Press, 1947.

ROSS, LILLIAN. *Portrait of Hemingway*. New York: Simon & Schuster, 1961.

ST. JOHN, ROBERT. *This Was My World* (Oak Park). New York: Doubleday, 1953.

SAMUELS, LEE. *A Hemingway Check List*. New York: 1951.

SANDERSON, S. F. *Ernest Hemingway*. New York: Grove Press, 1961.

SANFORD, MARCELLINE HEMINGWAY. *At the Hemingways*. Boston: Little, Brown & Co., 1961.

SLOCOMBE, GEORGE. *The Tumult and the Shouting*. New York: Macmillan, 1936.

STEFFENS, LINCOLN. *Autobiography of Lincoln Steffens*. New York: Harcourt, Brace, 1931.

STEIN, GERTRUDE. *The Autobiography of Alice B. Toklas*. New York: Random House, 1933.

TATE, ALLEN. "Random Thoughts on the Twenties." *The Minnesota Review*, Fall, 1960.

THOMAS, HUGH. *The Spanish Civil War*. New York: Harper and Brothers, 1961.

WARREN, ROBERT PENN. Introduction to Modern Standard Authors edition of *A Farewell to Arms*. New York: Scribner's, 1949.

YOUNG, PHILIP. "On Dismembering Hemingway." *Atlantic*, August, 1966. (a criticism of the controversial Hotchner book)

————. *Ernest Hemingway*. New York: Rinehart, 1952. Revised edition, 1965.

————. "Ernest Hemingway." *University of Minnesota Pamphlets on American Writers*, 1959.

Index